Who Is
R. L. Stine?

by M. D. Payne

illustrated by Jake Murray

Penguin Workshop

To Francesco, Gabe, and Josh, for letting a
Halloweenie into the world of Goosebumps—MDP

For Sara—here's to the many stories we've shared!
—JM

PENGUIN WORKSHOP
An Imprint of Penguin Random House LLC, New York

Text copyright © 2019 by M. D. Payne. Illustrations copyright © 2019 by Penguin Random House LLC. All rights reserved. Published by Penguin Workshop, an imprint of Penguin Random House LLC, New York. PENGUIN and PENGUIN WORKSHOP are trademarks of Penguin Books Ltd. WHO HQ & Design is a registered trademark of Penguin Random House LLC. Printed in the USA.

Visit us online at www.penguinrandomhouse.com.

Library of Congress Cataloging-in-Publication Data is available upon request.

ISBN 9780399539596 (paperback)   10 9 8 7 6 5 4 3 2 1
ISBN 9780399539602 (library binding)   10 9 8 7 6 5 4 3 2 1

Contents

Who Is R. L. Stine?

In 1990, R. L. Stine was a successful author. He had already written a best-selling series called Fear Street. Young adults loved his spooky stories. But he wondered if he could write a series for even younger readers—something scary, but not too scary. R. L. Stine never began working until he had the perfect title. He thought day and night about what to call this new children's series, but the name just wasn't coming to him.

One morning, as he was reading the TV listings, R. L. saw an advertisement that said "It's Goosebumps Week on Channel 11!" And he thought that would be the perfect name for his new series: Goosebumps! He knew it was going to be something special.

Goosebumps was equal parts scary and funny. It combined ideas from Fear Street and all the other scary stories, funny magazines, and silly joke books he had created as a child.

By July 1992, the first book in the Goosebumps series, *Welcome to Dead House*, was in bookstores. And children around the world loved it!

R. L. Stine's previous books had been popular, but nothing like this. At one point, his Goosebumps books were selling four million copies a month! The series grew into the biggest worldwide best seller of the 1990s. R. L. Stine worked as hard as he could. He became one of the most famous authors in the world and has written over three hundred books over the course of his career.

Along the way, the horrifying and hilarious Goosebumps tales have inspired children to read—and to read more! Many fans race to check as many titles off their reading wish lists as they can. The series has been featured on television, in film, onstage, at sleepovers, in backyards, and around campfires all over the world.

CHAPTER 1
A Totally Typical Family

Robert Lawrence Stine was born in Columbus, Ohio, on October 8, 1943. Bob, as he was called by his friends and family, was the first of three children. His brother, Bill, was born three years later. His sister, Pam, was born seven years later, in 1950.

His father, Lewis, worked for a restaurant-supply company. His mother, Anne, was a stay-at-home mom. In the city of Columbus, the Stine family lived in the wealthy neighborhood of Bexley. But their home was close to the railroad tracks—not where the really rich families lived.

Growing up in a town where most of the other kids had more money was tough for Bob— sometimes he felt as if he didn't fit in.

But Lewis and Anne always made sure their children got the best education they could, and gave them everything they needed. Bob was even able to go away to camp in the summer.

Bob and Bill shared a bedroom. Before bedtime, the brothers would tell each other scary stories. Bob's stories were usually about a younger boy who was a lot like Bill. When Bob got to the scariest part, he would end the story quickly. Bill was left wondering what terrifying thing might have happened to the kid in the story!

Bob would often get in trouble with his mother for spending too much time listening to the radio. In the early 1950s, not every home had a television set. Most people still listened to the radio for news reports, music, and entertaining story series, sometimes called "serials." Bob liked *The Lone Ranger*, *The Shadow*, *The Whistler*, and *Gang Busters*. These were continuing stories with new episodes each week. Bob learned how to be a better storyteller by listening to all these radio shows. But he was too scared to listen to the show called *Suspense*, because the voice that narrated the show was so terrifying.

Radio also connected Bob with the world outside Columbus, Ohio. Most of the shows he listened to were broadcast from New York City. And Bob dreamed of moving there one day.

He was a big fan of comic books, too. Bob discovered whole new worlds inside their pages. Although his mother had banned comic books from the house, Bob had found a sneaky way to read them: His barber kept a stack in the barbershop, so Bob would get a haircut every week just to read the comics! EC Comics were his favorites.

EC Comics

Entertaining Comics, known as EC Comics, published scary horror-themed comic books. Tales from the Crypt and The Vault of Horror were two of their popular series. They gave readers chills with titles like *The Thing from the Grave*, *Scared to Death!*, and *Rats Have Sharp Teeth!* The comics were filled with both funny and frightening stories. They were known for their twist endings that readers never guessed were coming. But many adults thought the comics were too gory and too violent.

In 1954, the US Senate declared that such scary horror comics were bad for children. EC's horror comic series were soon canceled. But EC continued publishing *MAD*, one of their funniest comics, as a magazine. *MAD* magazine became a huge influence on other funny magazines and comics that would follow.

But Bob wasn't happy just *reading* comics. He wanted to create his own funny and scary stories.

The Stines lived in a big, old house with many rooms, a basement, and an attic. Bob and Bill loved exploring the attic, and one day when he was seven, Bob was lucky enough to find an old typewriter there. As soon as he found it, he started to type up stories and jokes. He'd peck away at his work one letter at a time, with just one finger.

When he was nine, Bob created his first full magazine: *The All New Bob Stine Giggle Book*. It was much smaller than a regular magazine, but it was packed with jokes, riddles, and illustrations he had drawn to go along with the words.

He went on to create a series of magazines with titles like *Tales to Drive You Batty, Stine's Line*, and *HAH, For Maniacs Only!!* Bob's family had just bought their first TV, and his handmade magazines made fun of some of the TV shows he watched, just like the *MAD* comics he loved. He used not only the typewriter he had found in the attic but also pens, pencils, crayons, tape, glue, scissors, and a stapler. It was hard work, but being able to share his art and words with his brother and classmates, and to hear them laugh, was well worth it.

Bob wrote *so much*, in fact, that he rarely went outside. His parents would knock on his bedroom door and tell him to go out and play

with his friends. But Bob was very shy. No matter what other kids wanted to do (or what his parents said), he would rather stay in his room, writing and drawing. Bob didn't mind observing what other people were doing from a distance. He was

paying close attention to the world around him so that he could write stories in a very realistic way—a way that was actually quite funny.

Bob also stuck close to home because he wasn't really adventurous. When it was his turn to jump into the pool at summer camp like the other kids, he was too scared to do it. He wasn't very good at sports. And he even stayed away from his own garage after dark because he thought there was a monster hiding inside.

He was happy to stay safe in his room, typing away. For a kid in grade school, he worked very hard at putting together his magazines. And all that hard work was already starting to pay off.

CHAPTER 2
Make 'Em Laugh!

Bob kept writing throughout grade school and into middle school. He continued swapping spooky stories with his brother, Bill. When the family moved to a new house, the boys made an odd discovery in the woods behind their backyard: a small hill of strange, smooth white stones. Bob and Bill thought that the pile of stones

was somehow haunted. Soon, the stories they told had all their friends convinced that someone was buried under the stones!

Although he was great at telling scary stories, Bob was even more interested in making his friends laugh. He'd write joke books and bring them to school. The books were so funny that his classmates spent more time laughing than listening to their teachers. Once again, Bob was asked to stop writing—this time by his teachers!

For his first funny magazine series in middle school, *From Here to Insanity*, Bob created seven complete issues. This was the first time Bob used both sides of the paper. He proudly shared each issue with his classmates.

Bob only ever made one copy of each magazine, so that copy was passed around from person to person at school. Bob's magazines were so popular in class that he wrote a whole article on what to do if your teacher caught you reading

his magazine. It was a super-funny joke, until his teacher caught one of his friends reading that very article. The teacher was not happy and sent Bob to the principal. But Bob was always a good student who got As and Bs, so his teachers didn't

stay mad at him. And he did participate in other school activities. Bob tried to play clarinet in the marching band. But when he realized he couldn't walk and play at the same time, he became a singer in the school chorus instead.

When he wasn't making funny magazines, Bob was watching movies with Bill. Every Saturday afternoon they'd head to the theater to see horror films like *Creature from the Black Lagoon* and

It Came from Beneath the Sea. Bob was never terrified. "I think horror is funny," Bob said. "Horror makes me laugh in a movie theater."

In high school, Bob and his friend Jeff both had huge reel-to-reel tape recorders that they would use to record their made-up jokes and funny stories. Jeff also had a driver's license, so the boys would drive around town having fun.

Reel-to-reel tape recorder

When Bob got *his* license, his car wasn't nearly as nice as Jeff's or anyone else's in town—something that embarrassed Bob when he had to pick up his girlfriend for a date. But he didn't let it hold him back.

Bob kept on doing what he loved to do most. Throughout high school, he made magazines with names like *Eloquent Insanity* and *Uproarious Utopia*. He also enjoyed his writing assignments for school. He won several prizes for his essays. And he wrote the skit that the graduating students performed. It got huge laughs, from kids *and* adults. The first place Bob was ever published— aside from his own hand-drawn magazines—was in his school's newspaper.

Bob spent a lot of time writing and reading. He really liked science fiction and fantasy books.

 Stories like *Mindswap* carried him away to another world and time. But the first book that really scared Bob was *Something Wicked This Way Comes* by Ray Bradbury, which he read when he was nineteen.

Ray Bradbury (1920–2012)

Ray Bradbury wrote over six hundred short stories, twenty-seven novels, and many scripts for movies and television. He is best known for his science fiction and horror stories. Some of his most famous books are

Fahrenheit 451 and *The Martian Chronicles.*

Something Wicked This Way Comes, published in 1962, tells the story of two thirteen-year-old boys who explore the mysterious traveling carnival that has come to their small town.

Ray Bradbury's writing has influenced many people, from award-winning film director Steven Spielberg to popular horror author Stephen King.

CHAPTER 3
Jovial Bob

After graduating from high school, Bob was accepted to Ohio State. While he attended college, he lived at home with his family. He was happy that he could still enjoy his mother's cooking. He was *not* so happy that his "college roommate" was his younger brother, Bill.

Bob studied English at Ohio State. But he was most excited about the school's humor magazine, called the *Sundial*. Some famous writers and artists had started their careers at the *Sundial*— like humor writer James Thurber and comic strip artist Milton Caniff.

Bob had always dreamed of becoming the magazine's editor. An editor didn't write every article, like Bob had for his own projects, but made sure that other writers had their articles in on time and that there was enough material (art and articles) to fill each issue. The editor made all the final decisions.

Bob got the job, and editing the *Sundial* took up all his time. He joked that "every once in a while, I would go to class." He worked hard to make the magazine something his fellow students couldn't wait to read. Bob also published his own stories using his pen name (the name he used as a writer) "Jovial Bob," because he thought the new name would help the magazine do well. *Jovial* means happy or cheerful.

Jovial Bob made sure the magazine was filled with hilarious articles that made fun of every part of college life. Bob also knew how to publicize, or bring attention to, the magazine. In his senior year, he ran for student senate president—even though seniors weren't allowed to run—with the slogan "Elect a Clown for President." Even though the school didn't let him put his name on the ballot, Bob still got 1,163 votes out of the 8,727 total!

The *Sundial* was a huge success with the kids

at Ohio State. In 1965, it was voted the number one college humor magazine in the United States. Ohio State's 1965 yearbook stated: "Under the leadership of Editor 'Jovial' Bob Stine, the *Sundial* staff produced a new-sized magazine that hit a record high for circulation in *Sundial*'s fifty-three-year history." This meant that more students were buying and reading the *Sundial* than at any other time.

In June 1965, Bob graduated with a degree in English. He had learned many lessons editing and writing the *Sundial*. He had learned how to come up with new ideas fast. And he had learned how to work with other writers and illustrators to make the best magazine possible.

He wanted to move to New York City to continue the writing and editing he loved. There was only one problem: Bob didn't have enough money to make the move he'd always dreamed about. He had to find a job and start saving.

Bob became a substitute teacher. After a while, he was given his own class: middle-school history! His students didn't seem to like history (Bob didn't, either), so he had to think of an interesting way to get the class excited. His solution: free-reading day! If the students behaved and paid attention from Monday through Thursday, they could read whatever they wanted—even comic books!—on Friday.

Even while he was teaching, Bob was writing in his spare time. He wrote scripts for a radio show he called *Captain Anything*. Bob wrote it as a two-minute show about a superhero who could change into anything he wanted: a turtle, a chair, a rock, a wolf . . . anything! But the superhero's glasses always stayed, no matter what he transformed into. Unfortunately, no radio station was interested in airing his show. Radio shows had become less popular because by then many people had televisions.

Bob was a teacher for just one year, but it was an important year for him. The experience taught him a lot about middle-schoolers: how they talked, what they wore, and what they were interested in.

Most important, when the school year ended, Bob had enough money to finally make his move to New York City.

CHAPTER 4
A Tough Start

In the fall of 1966, Bob arrived in New York City. It was everything he hoped for and more. The city was bustling with more people than Bob had ever seen before. New York was packed with creative industries like television, advertising, publishing, recording, and the theater. And on every corner, there seemed to be talented writers and illustrators sitting at cafés and browsing in bookstores.

Bob rented the cheapest apartment he could find in the middle of Greenwich Village. He lived in a small one-room apartment with a tiny kitchen. He couldn't afford to eat anything more than bologna sandwiches. New York was an expensive town, and he had to find a job fast.

Greenwich Village

Greenwich Village (say: GREN-itch), on the west side of lower Manhattan, is one of the oldest neighborhoods in New York City. It is an artistic and historic neighborhood filled with homes and businesses that are older and smaller than in the rest of the city. The people who live there call it simply "the Village."

In the 1960s, the Village was an important neighborhood for artists and many other creative people. Clubs and theaters there hosted poets, musicians, and actors who drew audiences from all over the city and beyond. The center of the Village is Washington Square Park—a favorite spot of students from the two colleges in the Village: New York University and the New School.

New York was the center of the magazine-
publishing industry, and Bob wanted to work
at one of the more famous magazines like *Life*,

Esquire, or the *New Yorker*. He read all the classified ads—the newspaper sections that listed available jobs—but he didn't find anything that interested him.

He finally got an interview with a financial magazine called *Institutional Investor*. And Bob got the job. But he didn't know anything about the business of investing money. And he knew even less about what his actual job responsibilities were. He was fired on his first day!

Bob began to wonder if he would ever become successful as a writer in New York City. He felt as if the city were saying no to him! But he was determined to stick with it.

One day, he had a meeting with an editor who published magazines for teenagers. She offered him a job writing celebrity interviews for one hundred dollars a week—a great start! Bob knew that he could do the work. But he worried because he was getting paid to make things up: The interviews were all fake! His editor assured him that most superstars would be happy just to be written about. So, Bob quickly got to work writing dozens of made-up interviews each month. They were about celebrities like the Beatles, the Rolling Stones, and Diana Ross.

It was a strange job, but Bob proved he could work quickly no matter what he was writing— and he was finally getting paid.

While he was busy making up interviews,

another exciting opportunity came his way. His editor's boss launched a magazine called *Adventures in Horror*, and Bob was asked to write for it! His time was split between writing fake interviews and writing horror stories. But just as things began picking up, both the teen and horror magazines went out of business. Bob was out of a job.

Bob barely had enough money left to pay his rent. He found a new job at *Soft Drink Industry* magazine. It was written for the people who sell soda and everything used to make soda—from the syrup to the cans.

The work was boring, but Bob was writing—
something that always made him happy. He still
hoped to find an exciting job at a well-known
magazine. He wished he could make a living
writing something funny like the *Sundial* and the
magazines he had made as a kid.

During his breaks at *Soft Drink Industry*
magazine, Bob read classified ads, hoping to find
his dream job. While he was searching for that,
Bob found love. He met Jane Waldhorn, who was
also a writer, at a friend's party.

Bob said it was the luckiest night of his life—but it almost didn't happen. Bob didn't want to go. He was too shy! When he arrived at the party, Jane had a terrible cold. It didn't matter—Bob and Jane fell in love and got engaged a few weeks later. Bob still had to find the right job, but now he wasn't alone in New York City. Things were looking up.

CHAPTER 5
Going *Bananas*

In December 1968, Bob's job search was finally over. He was hired by the children's publisher Scholastic, Inc. His first job was writing news and history articles for *Junior Scholastic*, a current-events magazine for kids.

Scholastic published new magazines each week. Just like at his very first jobs in New York, Bob continued learning how to write very quickly. While he worked at Scholastic, Bob also learned to write for children in a way that connected with them—even children who weren't that interested in reading.

Scholastic, Inc.

Founded in 1920 by Maurice Robinson, Scholastic is an international company that publishes books, magazines, and educational materials for children in kindergarten through twelfth grade. It also produces audiobooks, television series, movies, teacher guides, and more.

Scholastic is known for its book clubs, which send Scholastic Book Club flyers to schools all across the United States. They also run book fairs, which deliver books directly to schools for children to buy.

Scholastic is the publisher of some of the world's most popular book series, including Harry Potter, Goosebumps, Clifford the Big Red Dog, and The Hunger Games.

Like Bob, Jane had recently started working at Scholastic, for the magazine *Scope*. Bob and Jane were married on June 22, 1969.

After *Junior Scholastic*, Bob worked on many other magazines for readers of all ages, including *Scholastic Search* (which focused on social studies) and *Wheels* (which helped teenagers who were learning how to drive). Bob learned about all kinds of subjects while writing for the magazines.

But even though Bob was becoming a better and faster writer, he was still writing for magazines that had been founded by other people. He wanted to have a magazine of his own—and he wanted it to be funny.

In 1975, Bob was asked to create and edit his own humor magazine for kids. Finally, his dream was coming true! Bob thought *Bananas* was a great name for the magazine. *Bananas* lived up to its name. It was filled with activities, comics, and funny advice columns. *Bananas* also had interviews

with the biggest stars of music, film, and television. (Although this time, all the interviews were real!) Bob worked as hard as he could on the magazine, and kids rushed to read each issue as soon as it was available.

Interview with the band KISS in *Bananas* magazine

Bob was having the time of his life at work, and it showed! He took his job as the office funnyman very seriously. He even had a rubber chicken hanging in his office. In addition to writing for the magazine, Bob wrote fake memos and sent them around to his friends at Scholastic.

He thought his coworkers would just laugh at how silly they were. But some actually believed that they were real—even the memo to wear a jacket because of a "test of the sprinkler system!"

While working on *Bananas*, Bob wrote his first book for kids, called *How to Be Funny*, in 1978. It was filled with silly tips and advice on different ways to be funny. Unfortunately, it was a flop. At his first book signing, Bob wore rabbit ears to be extra silly, and only one person bought a copy for him to sign.

But it didn't really matter to Bob. He was just happy living his dream of being a humor writer and the editor of *Bananas*.

CHAPTER 6
Writing Everything

In 1980, Bob and his wife, Jane, were working on two of the most popular kids' magazines in the country. Jane was the editor of *Dynamite*. Bob was still editing *Bananas*. And they had a baby boy, Matthew.

A few years after Matthew was born, however, *Bananas* was suddenly canceled. Bob couldn't believe it. He was shocked! Scholastic gave Bob another magazine to edit, *Maniac*, but one year later, it was canceled as well. After Bob left his job at Scholastic, he quickly moved his writing career in a different direction.

Bob began a new phase of his career, as a stay-at-home dad who wrote children's books. He and Matthew explored New York City together. They went to the American Museum of Natural History, watched movies, and played ball in the

park. And when he wasn't busy with Matthew, Bob was even busier with his writing.

Bob took on every book project that came his way, working with the same speed and humor he'd perfected during his sixteen years at Scholastic.

He wrote G.I. Joe action stories. He wrote Indiana Jones novels and James Bond Junior novels. He wrote over one hundred joke books with titles like *101 Silly Monster Jokes* and *Bored with Being Bored.* He wrote *Zero Heroes* bubble gum cards (trading cards that were packed with bubble gum)  featuring heroes like Caped Cucumber, Captain Forgetful, and Garlic Girl. He wrote the stories inside Mighty Mouse and Bullwinkle coloring books. He wrote anything and *everything*!

Bob even wrote books based on the Marvel Comics series Madballs—the story of rubber

balls with hideous faces and names like Dusty Dustbrain, Wolf Breath, and Horn Head who battle Dr. Frankenbeans. Bob has said that Madballs was his "lowest achievement." But he never said no to any new project!

While Bob was busy writing at home, his wife, Jane, and her friend Joan Waricha created their own publishing company, Parachute Publishing.

Jane edited many of Bob's books. Although Parachute Publishing did publish some of his books, they also presented some to even bigger companies to publish. Bob was about to take on a new project that would keep Jane and Joan's new company very, very busy!

CHAPTER 7
It All Started with a *Blind Date*

One day, Bob was having lunch with a friend, Jean Feiwel. Jean was an associate publisher at Scholastic. She thought Bob could write a scary book for teens. During lunch, Jean said, "Go home and write a book called *Blind Date*."

Bob had been writing funny books and magazines for a while. He hadn't thought of writing anything like a horror story. However, Bob never said no to a writing assignment. He told Jean he would do it.

He read other horror stories for teens by authors like Joan Lowery Nixon, Christopher Pike, and Lois Duncan. He thought back to the comics he had read in Tales from the Crypt, the ghost stories that he and his brother used to tell, the scary voice from *Suspense*, and all the horror movies he had watched. Then he crafted a terrifying tale about a boy who gets a phone call from a mysterious girl, claiming to be his blind date. But she isn't, really. In fact, she's not even alive!

Bob knew that "Jovial Bob Stine" wasn't a good pen name for the author of such a scary story. So he used the initials of his first and middle names and published the book as "R. L. Stine."

When *Blind Date* arrived in bookstores in

1986, it connected with his young readers in a way that his humor books hadn't. It was a huge success! After *Blind Date*, Scholastic asked Bob to write two more books: *Twisted* and *The Babysitter*. Both were also best sellers, and Bob started getting letters from readers asking for more spooky stories.

Bob could see that he was really on to something. He came up with the idea to write an entire series of spine-tingling horror books. He spoke with Jane and Joan at Parachute Publishing about his idea. They thought it was fantastic, so Bob went home to come up with a title. That's how Fear Street, a horror series for teens, was born.

The New Girl, the first book in the Fear Street series, was published in 1989, and it was an instant best seller! So were the next two books in the series: *The Surprise Party* and *The Overnight*.

Bob's horror titles were exactly the kinds of stories teenagers loved to read. Soon, Bob was writing one 176-page Fear Street book a month—that was pretty fast work!

But even with the success of Fear Street, Bob took on another new project. He worked as cocreator and head writer of the children's television show *Eureeka's Castle*. The show followed the quirky and hilarious characters that lived in a giant's windup toy castle. Bob created all the puppet characters, including Magellan, a friendly dragon with an uncontrollable tail who was always sneezing, and Batly, a clumsy bat who needed to wear glasses because he was nearsighted. The show premiered in 1989 on the Nickelodeon channel.

What's in a Name?

For each of his books, Bob always thought up the perfect title first. He then very carefully plotted out every chapter in an outline before he started writing.

Many of the titles Bob thought up were influenced by the movies that he and his brother had seen in theaters when they were young.

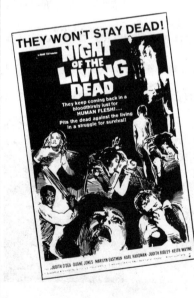

Actual Movie Title	R. L. Stine Book Title
Night of the Living Dead	Night of the Living Dummy
Invasion of the Body Snatchers	Invasion of the Body Squeezers, Parts 1 and 2
Revenge of the Creature	Revenge of the Lawn Gnomes
The Abominable Snowman	The Abominable Snowman of Pasadena
The Little Shop of Horrors	Little Comic Shop of Horrors
It Came from Beneath the Sea	It Came from Beneath the Sink!

Writing for television was unlike anything Bob had ever done before. He was used to writing on his own. But writing for TV involved a writer and many other people. Bob had to work with actors, directors, producers, and puppeteers before everyone could agree that Bob's ideas and scripts were "final."

He even became the editor of *Nickelodeon Magazine* for their first few issues. He always said yes to new projects. And with each new creative project, Bob learned more about writing—and about what made his young audience happy.

Nickelodeon

In 1979, Nickelodeon became the first cable-television channel for children. Cable television was new, and not many people were watching it. But by 2016, the station—also known as Nick—was one of the most popular channels, found in over ninety-two million homes in the United States.

Nick originated television shows like *SpongeBob SquarePants*, *PAW Patrol*, *iCarly*, *The Loud House*, and *Henry Danger*. The network also produces and awards the annual Kids' Choice Awards, where kids vote on the best of everything from movies and music to books and sports, and more.

CHAPTER 8
Goosebumps Break Out All Over!

At the start of the 1990s, Bob's spooky *Fear Street* was the best-selling young adult series in the country. He was the head writer for the wacky Nickelodeon series *Eureeka's Castle*. And, in its second season, the show won a CableACE award. By 1993, the series aired for three hours every weekday morning on Nickelodeon—that's fifteen hours of *Eureeka* a week!

Bob was a very busy writer! When Joan at Parachute Publishing asked Bob if he could come up with a series of scary books for a younger audience, he thought it was a good idea. He knew he could connect with grade-school kids by adding more of his sense of humor into his horror writing. Bob came up with the title Goosebumps. Parachute Publishing presented the series idea to Scholastic, where Bob had worked a decade before, and they agreed to publish the series.

At this point in his career, Bob was writing at a lightning-fast pace. He finished the first book in ten days. *Welcome to Dead House*, the story of two kids who have just moved into a haunted house, was published in July 1992 and was yet another instant best seller. Bob continued to write book after book: twenty-four titles a year! He wrote one book a month for the Goosebumps series and one for Fear Street. It was a good thing that Bob could write so fast.

Bob originally wrote Goosebumps for girls, because at that time everyone in publishing thought boys weren't as interested in reading. But he was getting just as much fan mail from boys as he was from girls. The series took off. Bob had been writing for twenty-five years. Although he had always found work as a writer, he had never become famous.

Readers all over the world couldn't get enough of the thrilling books that frightened them. Some titles were sold out as soon as they arrived at bookstores. And Bob kept coming up with new chills. Except for a few sequels, the kids and the monsters that terrorized them were new and different in each book. In *Monster Blood*, kids battle an evil ooze. In *Say Cheese and Die!*, kids find a camera that can make them disappear forever. And in *The Cuckoo Clock of Doom*—one of Bob's favorites—a kid accidentally sets time backward.

The Cuckoo Clock of Doom

Bob's monsters were strictly the stuff of nightmares, from mummies, vampires, and werewolves to special creations like a terrifying mask that can't be taken off (in *The Haunted Mask*) and a massive, smelly blob that sweats

Slappy

snails (in *The Horror at Camp Jellyjam*). His most famous villain is Slappy, an evil dummy who tries to make kids into his slaves while yelling nasty insults at them.

It seemed that Bob had created a magic formula to scare kids . . . but not scare them too much. He called it a "safe scare." He said that his stories are like roller coasters. When a rider is on the roller coaster, the speed and the steep drops can be frightening, but they know that when the ride comes to an end, they'll still be safe. His books were a perfect mix of horror and humor, along with plenty of twists and turns. His amazing use of a "cliff-hanger" at the end of each chapter made readers want to turn the page. A cliff-hanger is when an author ends a chapter right in the middle of a tense or scary situation, leaving the reader to wonder what will happen next—just like Bob left his brother wondering when he quickly ended a late-night story!

Bob also knew how to write characters that acted and sounded like real kids. It helped that he had a real kid at home. His son, Matthew, was twelve years old when Goosebumps was first published. Bob would also listen to what kids had to say during school visits, and he took the time to read his fan mail.

Goosebumps became the best-selling series ever—for children or adults. Suddenly, Bob was one of the most popular writers of all time.

Many things began to change in Bob's life. He had such huge book signings for Goosebumps that traffic stopped in cities as thousands of fans rushed to meet him. What a huge difference from his first book signing in 1978! Bob and his family were able to move into a much bigger apartment. It was a few miles uptown, but a world away from his tiny first apartment in New York City.

Bob's Office

Where does the author of such spooky stuff get his inspiration? From spooky stuff! Bob's office is filled with all sorts of scary things, including a life-size skeleton named Mr. Bones, a cockroach that is three feet long, and a pair of ventriloquist dummies—Slappy and a dummy version of Bob. Bob has also filled his office with things that make him laugh—like his pepperoni pizza clock.

His office walls are lined with books and a collection of old radios. And he's kept copies of the handmade funny magazines he put together when he was in school.

Bob spends six or seven days a week in his office. He starts writing first thing in the morning and keeps writing for as long as he can each day—usually through the afternoon.

CHAPTER 9
Worldwide Fame

R. L. Stine's success with Goosebumps was so unbelievable that many people couldn't explain how it happened—even Bob himself! He thought that his achievement felt kind of like winning the lottery—nearly impossible.

In 1995, at a time when Bob's new books were being bought by the *millions*, a Goosebumps series premiered on TV. It was the top children's show in the United States for three years in a row.

A Goosebumps attraction was built at Disney-MGM Studios—part of Walt Disney World—in 1997. It was called Goosebumps HorrorLand Fright Show and FunHouse. There has even been a live stage show, *Goosebumps Live on Stage*, from 1998 to 1999, and a musical, *Goosebumps the*

Musical: Phantom of the Auditorium, in theaters across the United States in 2016. A 4-D movie, *R. L. Stine's Haunted Lighthouse*, played at SeaWorld and Busch Gardens from 2003 to 2006.

Goosebumps has been turned into two comic-book series. In 2006, famous comic artists (from series like Batman and Justice League) brought Bob's books to life in Goosebumps Graphix. IDW Comics created all-new stories based on Goosebumps in 2017 (Monsters at Midnight) and 2018 (Download and Die!).

Kids played Goosebumps board games and video games. They could buy Goosebumps

T-shirts, dolls . . . even boxer shorts and Goosebumps fake blood!

But not all the attention was good. Some parents thought that the books were too scary for younger readers. (The series is written for eight- to twelve-year-olds.) Some critics actually thought that Bob was a bad writer! Goosebumps was listed as the fifteenth-most-challenged book of the 1990s by the American Library Association. (A book is "challenged" when parents ask to have it removed from libraries.)

No matter how many parents or critics didn't like his books, Bob's loyal readers always came back for more. Kids told their friends about Goosebumps. And their friends would tell *their* friends. In the mid-1990s, Bob received over four hundred pieces of fan mail *each day* from readers, parents, teachers, and librarians.

Even after becoming the most popular author in the world, with Goosebumps and Fear Street,

Bob continued to create new book and television series.

In 2000, Bob started a new book series about kids' fears—The Nightmare Room. Readers could create their own stories on a Nightmare Room

website, and in 2001, a TV show based on the books was made. Each episode began with the voice of R. L. Stine growling, "Don't fall asleep, or you may find yourself in The Nightmare Room!" (The voice was not actually Bob's, but belonged to an actor playing him.)

In 2004, Bob wrote new spooky stories that were only about ghosts. Mostly Ghostly was his series about a boy named Max and the two young ghosts that live in his closet, Nicky and Tara. Nicky and Tara want Max to help them find their parents. If he helps them, they promise to solve all his problems (though they usually end up creating

more problems). Mostly Ghostly was also made into three movies for the Disney Channel.

Just one year later, the Rotten School series debuted. Rotten School wasn't scary like most of Bob's other books. It was much funnier, with stories such as *The Big Blueberry Barf-Off* and *Calling All Birdbrains*.

In 2010, a new television show thrilled his fans: *R. L. Stine's The Haunting Hour*. The show was based on Bob's short stories from *Nightmare Hour* (1999) and *The Haunting Hour: Chills in the Dead of Night* (2001), including "Afraid of Clowns," "Nightmare Inn," and "Alien Candy." The show was scarier than the *Goosebumps* TV show, but fans couldn't get enough! In the four seasons that the show was on the air, it won three Emmy Awards for Outstanding Children's Series.

His tremendous success has led Bob to become a writer for all ages. He's written two books for adults: *Superstitious* (1995) and *Red Rain* (2012). And he's written two picture books for younger children with illustrator Marc Brown, the creator of the Arthur books—*The Little Shop of Monsters* in 2015 and *Mary McScary* in 2017.

Bob has traveled all over the world to talk about writing and reading, heading as far away as Russia—at the invitation of First Lady Laura Bush in 2003—Australia, and China.

Goosebumps around the World

Chinese editions of Goosebumps books

The Goosebumps series has sold over four hundred million copies worldwide. It's been a best seller in the United States as well as in the United Kingdom, France, and Australia. The books have been translated into thirty-two languages and have sold over ten million copies in China alone! In fact, when Bob visited China, they gave him an honorary last name, *Kong Bu*, which means "scary."

The Goosebumps books are called *Escalofríos* (shaking skin) in Spanish, *Gänsehaut* (goose skin) in German, *Chair de poule* (flesh of the chicken) in French, and *Grillers* (creepy) in Afrikaans.

Goosebumps eventually made it from the small screen (television) to the big screen (movie theaters). On October 16, 2015, *Goosebumps*, the movie, premiered in theaters worldwide. And along with many of his favorite book characters, Bob himself made a very brief appearance in the movie as "Mr. Black." The star of the movie, Jack Black, played a character called R. L. Stine— though Jack played a not-so-nice version of Bob.

Jack Black in *Goosebumps*, the movie

Bob enjoyed the movie and thought it was the same perfect balance of funny and frightening that is found in his books. And the movie was a hit! The Goosebumps series—once again—climbed back onto the best-seller lists. The movie earned more than $150 million around the world and led to a sequel, *Goosebumps 2: Haunted Halloween*, in October 2018. Slappy was back and causing more trouble than ever.

CHAPTER 10
Never Say No!

Bob is a very busy man. But he always finds time to help children learn to read and write. In 1996, he established The R. L. Stine Writing Program in his hometown of Columbus, Ohio, and offered the program free to teachers around the country so they can help young people polish their writing skills.

In 2002, he won the first-ever Champion of Reading Award from the Free Public Library of Philadelphia—an award given to a person committed to helping other people read. In 2015, he donated digital copies of all his Goosebumps books to Worldreader—a company that sells books and uses their profits to help children around the world find a way to read, especially when they do not have the money to buy books.

Though Bob always knew he wanted to be a writer, he never dreamed how successful he would become. His book sales are well into the hundreds of millions and rising every day. Only the Harry Potter series has sold more copies.

Bob has also received three Nickelodeon Kids' Choice Awards, the International Thriller Writers Silver Bullet Award, the Horror Writers Association's Lifetime Achievement Award, and an Inkpot Award from Comic-Con, the biggest comics and entertainment convention in America.

Bob is the most popular writer of scary books for children, and he is often called "the Stephen King of children's books."

Even Bob has said, "I'm Stephen King for kids." But it wasn't until 2015 that Bob and Stephen finally met at an awards ceremony. They introduced their wives and spoke to each other about their writing. King joked that he was upset that Bob had already written about many of the best themes. And Bob later admitted, "I'm a real Stephen King admirer. . . . *Pet Sematary* . . . is the all-time creepiest!"

Stephen King (1947–)

American author Stephen King was born in 1947. As a young boy, he loved EC Comics and *Tales from the Crypt*. He often wrote stories for his brother's homemade newspaper.

Known as "the king of horror," he has sold over 350 million scary, mysterious, and suspenseful books for adults.

Stephen has written fifty-nine novels, over two hundred short stories, and six nonfiction works. He's won numerous awards, including the National Medal of Arts, presented to him by President Barack Obama. Many of his books have been made into movies, including *Carrie*, *The Shining*, *Cujo*, *It*, *Pet Sematary*, *Misery*, *Children of the Corn*, and *The Dark Tower*.

Bob continues to write new Goosebumps books—SlappyWorld is the latest series. And he still writes new Fear Street titles—because fans on Twitter have demanded them! Bob is an active Twitter user, tweeting about everything from writing to his favorite music.

In 2018, he edited a book of short stories from other authors called *Scream and Scream Again!* Each story began or ended with a scream!

After years of reading comic books, Bob finally wrote a few. In 2017, he got the chance to write a new series for a classic Marvel character called Man-Thing. In Bob's version of the comic, the "thing" is a  Hollywood movie monster who has to choose between fame and saving his swamp.

And Bob continues to travel around the United States, appearing everywhere from the bookstores and libraries of small towns to major events such as Comic-Con.

R. L. Stine has already created a huge universe of stories and characters that have wowed generations of children. He's sold nearly half a billion books in thirty-five languages! But Bob has said many times over that he will continue to write for as long as he can—pecking away with one finger, one key at a time, just like when he was a young boy using an old typewriter in his bedroom at home.

What will the author who never says *no* say *yes* to next?

Timeline of R. L. Stine's Life

1943	Born Robert Lawrence Stine on October 8 in Columbus, Ohio
1952	Creates his first funny magazine, *The All New Bob Stine Giggle Book*
1962	Becomes editor of the *Sundial*, the Ohio State University's humor magazine
1969	Marries Jane Waldhorn
1975	Creates his first professional humor magazine, *Bananas*
1978	Writes his first children's book, *How to Be Funny*
1980	Son, Matthew, is born
1986	Writes his first horror novel, *Blind Date*
1989	Fear Street series debuts
1992	Goosebumps series debuts
1995	Weekly *Goosebumps* TV show debuts
2001	*The Nightmare Room* TV series debuts
2004	Mostly Ghostly series debuts
2010	*R. L. Stine's The Haunting Hour* TV series debuts
2014	Wins Horror Writers Association's Lifetime Achievement Award
2015	*Goosebumps*, the movie, premieres
2017	Marvel Comics *Man-Thing* is published
2018	*Goosebumps 2: Haunted Halloween* premieres

Timeline of the World

1933 — *The Lone Ranger* radio program debuts

1941 — United States enters World War II

1945 — World War II ends

1950 — The first Tales from the Crypt comic book is published

1952 — *MAD* is first published as a comic book

1957 — Sputnik, the first artificial Earth satellite, is launched into space by the Soviet Union

1964 — The Beatles' first tour in the United States

1969 — First moon landing takes place

1977 — First fully assembled personal computers are sold

1986 — US space shuttle *Challenger* explodes upon takeoff

1989 — The Berlin Wall falls, ending the three decades of rivalry and tension between the United States and the Soviet Union known as the Cold War

1997 — The first Harry Potter book, *Harry Potter and the Philosopher's Stone*, is published in the United Kingdom

2000 — Y2K computer bugs fail to happen

2004 — Facebook is founded

2006 — Pluto is declared no longer a planet

2011 — Japan is struck by a 9.0-magnitude earthquake and tsunami

2018 — South Korea hosts the 2018 Winter Olympics

Bibliography

*Books for young readers

*Bowman, Chris. *R. L. Stine*. Minneapolis, MN: Bellwether Media, Inc., 2017.

*Cohen, Joel H. *R. L. Stine*. San Diego, CA: Lucent Books, Inc., 2000.

Lippman, Laura. "Giving Them Goosebumps," *Roanoke Times*, March 28, 1996.

*Parker-Rock, Michelle. *R. L. Stine: Creator of Creepy and Spooky Stories*. Berkeley Heights, NJ: Enslow Publishers, Inc., 2005.

*Purslow, Neil. *R. L. Stine*. New York: AV² by Weigl, 2014.

"RL Stine Interview with Writers Talk." Writers Talk. The Ohio State University's Center for the Study and Teaching of Writing. June 28, 2012. YouTube video, 21:22. https://www.youtube.com/watch?v=E5j96KaAUX4.

*Stine, R. L. *It Came from Ohio! My Life as a Writer*. New York: Scholastic, Inc., 2015.

Website

www.rlstine.com